Bengal Cats and Kittens

Complete Owner's Guide
To Bengal Cat and Kitten Care

Personality, temperament, breeding,
training, health, diet, life expectancy,
buying, cost, and more facts.

By Taylor David

Bengal Cats and Kittens
Complete Owner's Guide to Bengal Cat and Kitten Care
ISBN 978-1-927870-04-4

Author: Taylor David
Copyright © 2013 Ubiquitous publishing
ubiquitouspublishing.com
Published in Canada

Printed in the USA

Acknowledgements

I would like to thank my two children for inspiring me to write this book. As an owner of three Bengal cats over a decade, I found them to be such sweet, loyal, as well as spirited animals to have around. I can honestly attest to their exceptionally good fit for "dog people" like me wanting a cat with a dog-like personality.

I'd also like to extend my thanks to my spouse, who supports me in my every endeavor, and who was the person who convinced me to get my first Bengal kitten named Cody. I'm so glad I did.

Cody taught me so much about unconditional love between humans and cats that we ended up adding more Bengals to our family over the years. They have all provided quite a few laughs for us along the way with their fascinating personalities, enriching our lives tremendously.

Table of Contents

Foreword

In most people's minds, there are house cats and "big" cats. The latter get narrowed down to lions, tigers, and leopards in the popular perception. In reality, there are 37 species of wild cats distributed globally, with 30 of those considered "small."

One of the most common and widespread of these is the leopard cat (*felisbengalensis*.) They are found throughout southern and eastern Asia, including the Philippines and Indonesia.

This species, like many wild animals in the world today, suffers the effects of habitat destruction, but they are not considered in any immediate danger of extinction.

Scientifically, leopard cats are described as being the size of a "house cat," but with longer legs. Weight varies fairly widely by subspecies, however, so you can find 5 lb. (2.26 kg) leopard cats in the Philippines and 15 lb. (6.8 kg) specimens in the breed's northernmost ranges.

In coloration, these wild cats are anywhere from bright red to tawny brown with gray and golden tones in the middle of the spectrum. They tend to have white bellies, and their markings are prominent stripes, swirls, or rosettes.

All wild cats have beautifully defined lines on their faces. Their heads are small, but the eyes are large and luminous, highlighted by equally big ears that may or may not be tufted.

Wildlife biologists describe leopard cats as efficient small predators that, even in their wild state, can and do live in relative proximity to humans with complete peace. They are not overtly aggressive cats, and have a native curiosity that makes them open to some level of interaction with humans, albeit at a distance.

This is not to say that there are not well-documented cases of leopard cats that have been tamed and kept as pets. By the same token, some orphaned leopard cats that have been bottle fed and raised with humans, revert to their wild ways as they age and just slip away at the first chance, never to be seen again.

All of these qualities — the elusiveness, the superior abilities as a small hunter, the curiosity, the sheer beauty — have made these small cats an object of admiration and desire among cat fanciers for hundreds of years.

At the first organized cat show in London in 1871 there were already attempted hybrid crosses of leopard cats and domestic animals.

It was not, however, until the 1960s that a concerted breeding program with Asian Leopard Cats was undertaken as part of scientific research into the breed's immunity to feline leukemia. (For a full treatment of this story, please see Appendix I.)

What came out of that work, and the dedicated efforts of cat lovers that took up the breed's development, is the remarkable domestic cat called the Bengal.

Make no mistake. The cat that has earned the right to be called a Bengal is at least four generations removed from his wild ancestors. He is, in every way, a "house" cat, but one with a "wild" appearance, an unusually sharp mind, and an endearingly unique personality.

Looks, however, are the *only* thing wild about a Bengal.

Bengals were accepted as a new breed by The International Cat Association in 1986, and gained championship status in 1991. They are one of the most frequently exhibited of all TICA breeds today, and the object of dedicated and loving breeding programs around the world.

The goal of those programs is to create a docile house cat with rich markings and an arresting personality. Since show Bengals can be marked down for any sign of aggression, these cats are being selectively bred for the absolute best behavioral qualities.

The result is an inquisitive, active companion that comes roaring into your life filled with good-natured interest in everything you're doing and quite convinced his presence is a must in every facet of your day. If you don't want a constant and opinionated feline companion, don't get a Bengal.

If you do want a friend for life, one who will constantly entertain you with his antics — run, jumping, leaping, bounding, rolling, somersaulting, and climbing — not to mention splashing water all over the place — then the Bengal will be your dream cat.

With their soft, luxurious coats, conversational voices, and love of sleeping with their humans, Bengals are like no other breed — even surpassing the venerable Siamese for interactivity and devotion.

The poet and novelist Jean Cocteau said, "I love cats because I enjoy my home; and little by little, they become its visible soul."

Prepare to meet the Bengal — a breed like no other that will both win your heart, and enrich your home.

Chapter 1 - Introduction to the Bengal Breed

Cat fanciers have had an interest in "wild" breeds from the first cat show held in London in 1871 at the Crystal Palace to present day. The earliest mention of hybrid cats crossed with the small, 10 pound (4 kg) Asian Leopard Cat (ALC) was in 1889.

The true development of the breed known as the Bengal today, which derives from the ALC, stemmed from research into feline leukemia conducted by Dr. William Centerwall in the 1960s

(To understand the complete evolution of the Bengal breed, which is a long and involved genetic tale, please see

Appendix I - Detailed History and Development of the Bengal Breed.)

Today, the fully domesticated cats called Bengals, which are wild in appearance only, are at the very least F4 crosses, meaning they have an ALC great-great-grandparent. In many regions, any Bengal F3 and lower is still considered "wild" and subject to a variety of regulations.

(For a more complete understanding of filial degree, please see Appendix II - Filial Degree Explained.)

Similarity to Other "Wild" Species

Bengals are not the only "wild" domestic species. All are derived from a similar genetic mix to a small, wild breed, and are prized for their exotic looks and unique personalities.

Savannah

One of the newest of all cat breeds, the Savannah, results from crossing a common house cat with an African Serval. The result is a tall, slender cat with big ears that is often described as being a "house cheetah."

The Savannah is the largest of all domestic cats, weighing in at 20-30 pounds (9-13 kg). The breed was developed in the 1980s, and was not granted championship status by The International Cat Association (TICA) until 2012.

Chausie

The Chausie derives from the selective breeding of domestic cats with a Jungle Cat. Chausies, like Bengals, are active, fearless, devoted pets and, like the Savannah, they are long-legged and graceful.

With a powerful ability to run and jump, the Chausie is often referred to as the Olympic athlete of the cat world. Depending on their filial degree, a Chausie can weigh as much as 22 pounds (9 kg), although F4s for the breed drop into the 15 pound (6 kg) range.

Serengeti

The Serengeti was developed out of a desire to create a domestic cat with a likeness to the African Serval, but with less "wild" blood. Bengals were used in the development of this breed, and crossed with oriental shorthairs.

The result is a long-legged, medium-boned domestic cat with a short, tight coat and a distinct pattern of black spots on a yellow to gold background. Males weigh 10-15 pounds (4-6 kg) and females 8-12 pounds (3-5 kg).

Safari

The Safari cat is a rare hybrid created in the 1970s by crossing domestic cats with the South American Geoffroy's cat. They are unusual animals with the desired "wild" appearance, but with exceptionally affectionate natures.

The Safari's rarity is due to the difficulty in breeding the two species, which have differing numbers of chromosomes.

The resulting complication is that cats weighing 8-12 pounds (3-5 kg) can produce offspring that weigh in excess of 25 pounds (11 kg).

Physical Characteristics

Bengals not only have unique physical characteristics that lend them a "wild" appearance so appealing to fans of the breed, but they also have personalities that are unlike that of any other domestic cat.

Size

Truly domestic Bengals, who have an Asian Leopard Cat as a great-great-grandfather (or are even more removed from their wild origins) are medium sized cats.

Size does vary by the genetics of any pedigreed line, but on average, a male Bengal will weigh 12-15 pounds (5-6 kg). Females average 8-12 pounds (3-5 kg).

In terms of length, most Bengals are 22" or greater (roughly 56 cm).

Coat

Bengals have a dense, luxurious coat. It is soft to the touch, so much so that stroking one feels as if your fingers are literally melting into the pelt. A Bengal's fur can be stroked in any direction without resistance. On Bengals with exceptionally plush coats, the fur breaks at the neck.

Some Bengals have a recessive gene for a coat characteristic called "glitter." When air encircles the hair shafts in the pelts of these animals, it causes iridescent light refraction, which shimmers or glitters in sunlight. The effect is nothing short of spectacular.

Patterns

The Bengal's pattern flows horizontally, mimicking the look of its ALC ancestors. The dominant patterns are marbled swirls and large random spots or rosettes. (Typically, Bengals with marbling still display some rosettes.)

It's possible for Bengals to have white on their bellies, and on the back of the ears. The largest variation in coloration, however, lies in intensity. The most vivid contrasts are the most desirable.

The background color on the breed ranges from yellow to a bright rufous, with a muted charcoal in the middle of the tonal range. Spots range from jet black to brown and reddish tones.

Color Variations

In addition to the traditional colors, the following variations are accepted for the breed:

Snow Bengals - This coloration, also known as Seal Lynx Points, Seal Minks, or Seal Sepias are white, with contrasting colors in the nutmeg to pewter range. In this variation, blue eyes are possible, but the eyes may be green, gold, or copper. The kittens are born completely white and develop their mature coloring and pattern as they age.

Silver Bengal - These cats are the newest Bengal coloration to be accepted. The base coat is "clear" silver punctuated with pewter or ebony markings in the typical marbled or rosetted style. True Silver Bengals will have no "tarnish," which appears as a yellowing or browning of their coat. It's important to understand that in many respects, this breed is still being standardized and expanded, with some breeders even working on a long-haired variation.

The standard of any such variation is whether or not it will breed "true," meaning that both parents exhibit the trait and are capable of passing it on.

It is likely, given the rising popularity of the breed, that more variations will be accepted in years to come.

Rosette Styles

Bengals display six styles of rosette:

- embryonic - The spots show signs of a second color present.

- paw print - Each spot encircles another spot or a cluster of spots.

- donut - The rosettes look as if the centers are missing.

- arrowhead - The spots appear to point toward the back of the body.

- rosetted marble - Rosetting is present in the marble swirls.

- rosetted snow - The coat is lighter, with rosetted markings.

There is no pattern mixing. A Bengal will exhibit only one type of rosette.

Eyes

When Bengal kittens first open their eyes, they look black. At 9-10 weeks, they turn light blue. As the cat ages, its black eyeliner comes in, and the mature eye color appears, which will be green, gold, or copper. Only the "snow" variations have blue or aqua eyes.

In show cats, the deeper eyes with clear eyeliner are the most desirable. In conformation, the eyes should be large and rounded.

Ears

Bengals have small, well-rounded ears. They should be set as much on the top as on the sides of the head.

The Exceptional Bengal Personality

No one should ever adopt a Bengal without an understanding of the unique nature of these cats. They are unlike any other breed, and are endearing, quirky, intelligent, needy, demanding, vocal, loyal, and affectionate.

For some people, that bundle is too much with which to contend, and for others it makes for the absolute perfect cat.

Bengals have been described as dog like, and oftentimes they do get along better with dogs than with other cats. (If you have a Bengal in the house, he will be the alpha cat no matter what.)

Bengals happily play fetch, generally with no training whatsoever, and with a stamina and enthusiasm you will likely find exhausting.

In fact, Bengals are incredibly high energy and active. They love to climb — anything and everything — including you. Bengal kittens are known for scampering right up people's pants legs in their desire to interact. They'll chase anything and everything, including random flashes of light moving across the floor.

Any source of water is considered an object of fascination, which makes a Bengal very easy to bathe, but also a potential pest when it comes to splashing and making messes.

They howl when they're lonely, spanning an impressive vocal range, and they will talk back vociferously. (Don't even try to ignore a Bengal. It doesn't work.) Remember that a Bengal will be your constant, devoted companion, but he's also apt to be your supervisor. These cats simply cannot imagine that you don't want their presence and opinion at all times.

If you let a Bengal sleep with you at night — and it's very hard not to — don't expect to break the habit later on. A Bengal shut out of the bedroom will do just about anything to get back inside, including scratching insistently for as long as it takes to wear your resistance down.

Bengals are great with children, and amazingly tolerant, even patiently allowing their tails to be pulled, and keeping

their claws retracted. This is an interesting trait in a breed that can get aggressive, but their overall gentle natures seem to make room for a patient response with children.

They love to look at themselves in the mirror, and they love to mimic everything and anything you do. This can result in some difficult habits to accommodate, like your cat turning the lights on and off all night long.

You will need to be very careful what you teach your Bengal, because they don't forget, and they're perfectly capable of taking what they have learned and extrapolating the behavior.

What you get in return for this quirkiness, however, is a cat that has a capacity for unparalleled devotion. You cannot leave a Bengal alone. They do suffer from separation anxiety.

They're will retaliate if bored or anxious, shredding furniture or even spraying. But when they are with their humans, the only place they truly want to be, there is simply no more devoted breed of cat.

If you want an absolute four-legged friend for life, and you are prepared to offer that level of friendship in return, then a Bengal is the cat for you.

Common Misconceptions About the Bengal

Because the Bengal has a wild appearance, they are often regarded as something of the "pit bull" of the cat world, and are associated with all kinds of presumed negative behavioral traits.

It is crucial to understand that Bengals who are F4 or later are *completely domestic cats*. They do not, as a breed, retain primitive characteristics.

Perhaps the most definitive way to put this issue to bed is to point out that Bengals are actively being bred for good temperament for a highly specific reason, as explained by Dr. Solveig Pfluegar, Director of Laboratory Genetics at Bay State Medical Center, Western Campus of Tufts University of Medicine and the Chair of the International Cat Association (TICA) Genetics Committee:

"SBT Bengal's are not more prone to having behavioral problems than other breeds of cats. I'm a cat judge for TICA and TICA rules states that you cannot call a cat a Bengal until the third generation.

The Bengal cat being shown and registered has at least three generations of pedigree and is a very nice domesticated pet. The credit should go to responsible breeders who have worked hard to get a good personality in the Bengal breed."

Dr. Pfleuger goes on to explain that judges at TICA cat shows disqualify Bengals for difficult or combative behavior like paw swatting at a judge. "The show standard is unique in TICA toward Bengal's. Any inappropriate display of behavior results in that Bengal being disqualified.

Bengal breeders are motivated to breed cats and to bring cats to the show ring who are nice cats."

(Source for Dr. Pfleuger's remarks: "Common Misconceptions," http://wildexpressions.ca/bengal/the-bengal/what-is-a-bengal/common-misconceptions/ , Accessed June 2013.)

Chapter 2 - Buying a Bengal Cat

There are two crucial steps involved in buying a Bengal.

- Understanding that you are not buying an "ordinary" cat.

- Finding a reputable breeder. (This does NOT mean going to the classified section of the newspaper.)

There are certainly a few things to know before you bring a Bengal into your life, but they come with an important caveat — your Bengals will continue to surprise you throughout their lives.

What to Know Before You Adopt a Bengal

Many people who have owned cats before don't realize that in owning a Bengal they are literally bringing a life *force* home. These cats are extremely intelligent, highly active, and when they want your attention, uniquely demanding.

Highly Vocal When They Want Something

When a Bengal really wants to be heard, he howls — conversationally, discordantly, across multiple octaves, with an occasional gurgle thrown in for good measure. Their voices are like no cat you've ever heard before.

The first time your Bengal really lets loose, you'll be convinced the neighbors, three doors down can hear every yowl.

Loving and Loyal

If Bengals can be demanding, they don't do so without giving something back. They have an almost phenomenal capacity to love their humans, and their loyalty is absolute and complete.

A Bengal is not the typical "independent" or "aloof" feline. They want time with you. They get very lonely without you. And they usually come when they're called.

If these cats are noisy and opinionated once they show up, it's only because they simply cannot conceive that you do not want their input and guidance on every facet of your life.

Love Gadgets

Depending on your interpretation, it's either a charming trait or a potential disaster that Bengals have a love of gadgets. Some Bengals have a strong tendency to become fixated. Once they learn to flip an electrical switch, there's no stopping them.

Because they're so smart, Bengals think all technology is just a higher level of cat toy. This extends to turning on TV sets and changing channels, opening the drawer on the DVD player, and doing absolutely unspeakable things to the computer if you're foolish enough to leave it on and unattended.

Play in Water

Unlike most cats, Bengals love to play in the water. They'll get in the shower with you, figure out how to turn on the sink, splash in their bowl, and quite happily fish in the aquarium.

Will Always Be the Dominant Cat

If you bring a Bengal into a household with other cats, no matter how much larger or older those cats might be, the Bengal will always be the dominant cat.

They are highly territorial, and predatory. If your neighbors have a fish pond, your Bengal will not only go for a swim, but he'll bring a fish home to you as a present. Expect lots of "trophy" birds, presented at your feet with an expectant, upturned look that clearly says, "Look what I did!"

Loyalty of Litter Mates

While this is true of almost any breed of cat, two Bengals that are raised together from kittenhood will have an incredible bond. This level of "bestie" status can go a long way toward alleviating any kind of separation anxiety.

On the flip side, however, Bengals who lose their close companion actively grieve, suffering real pain and depression at the loss of their friend.

Highly Trainable

Due to the exotic looks, their predatory ways, and their extensive climbing skills, it's really best to keep your Bengal indoors for its safety. The great thing about this breed is that they are highly trainable, and an easily be taught to walk well on a leash.

Since they're also highly people-oriented, walk time quickly becomes the highlight of your Bengal's day. Throw in a dangling toy on a wand for some acrobatic, predatory, leaping and tumbling out in the yard, and you're going to have one happy cat on your hands.

This propensity to be trained is almost limitless. Some owners have even successfully taught their Bengals to use the toilet. It's just a matter of time and patience — and not a lot is required of either one, because theses cats catch on fast and have a great time with the whole learning process because they're doing it with you.

Where Bengals are Banned and Why

Bengals, like other non-domestic source hybrid cats (Chausie, Serengeti, Savannah, or Safari) may be legally banned or restricted by local or regional governments. These regulations are often vague and imprecise, based on the presumption, in most cases, that these cats are "wild."

The perceived level of "danger" may be different in relation to the cat's generational status (please see Appendix II - Filial Degree Explained.)

In general, the farther a Bengal is genetically removed from its wild ancestor, the less likely that the cat will be be subject to regulation. A license may or may not be required, but vaccination laws will definitely apply.

(Please see Appendix III - Bengal Cats and Legal Considerations for more specific details.)

Locating and Working with a Breeder

As you are familiarizing yourself with the breed, it's a good idea to attend cat shows and talk to Bengal breeders. This will give you an opportunity to see the kind of animals they raise, and to find sources for Bengal kittens in your area.

If you cannot attend a cat show, try the home page of The International Bengal Cat Society at BengalCat.com. This group is the oldest and most extensive group dedicated to the Bengal breed.

Founded in 1988, all breeders who are TIBCS affiliated are required to sign a Code of Ethics governing the manner in which they offer kittens for sale.

The Society maintains a breeder directory, complete with contact information and website links.

A secondary source for breeder information is The International Cat Association at Tica.org.

Evaluating the Breeder

It's important to evaluate the facility in which your Bengal was born and where it has experienced the first weeks of its life.

- Is the facility clean?
- Are the animals happy and in good health?
- What kind of language does the breeder use? Be wary of breeders that use phrases like "miniature tiger" or "little leopard."

You want a breeder who is most interested in finding out about *you*. If you don't feel like you're being interviewed as a suitable parent, something is wrong.

Age at Adoption

Good breeders don't let kittens leave the cattery before they are at least 13 weeks of age. Earlier than that, the cat will likely exhibit behavioral problems like wool sucking (nursing inanimate objects like blankets or even their human's ear lobe).

Additionally, kittens should be eating solid food and they should be litter box trained. Bengal kittens that have not been weaned may be difficult to feed, refusing anything but kitten formula.

If this happens with an older kitten, use a little smoked salmon or even cheap sardines to entice the kitten's appetite. This is also a good trick when an adult cat is sick and won't eat. Cats won't eat what they can't smell, so when a cat isn't eating, go for something stinky.

Questions to Ask the Breeder

During the negotiation phase with the breeder, and at the point at which you meet the kittens for the first time, there will be some information you'll want to make sure you get.

- Ask about the kitten's parents.
You'll not only want to know if the parents are in good health, but its good policy to see some certification of that fact. If possible, meet the parents.

Try to get a sense of their personality, and how they interact with the kittens. Some Bengal mothers are extremely over protective, especially if their kittens are very young.

- Find out about early life healthcare.

What vaccinations has the kitten received? Has it been dewormed? What conditions (including potential genetic defects) has it been evaluated for?

Have any of the other kittens in the litter been sick?(If so, consider not adopting from the cattery in question since feline diseases are highly contagious.)

Is the kitten flea free? (This is not only important from a health standpoint, but it can take weeks to get rid of a flea infestation!)

- Investigate socialization.

How have these kittens been socialized? Is it comfortable being handled? All kittens are reticent around strangers for a few minutes, and then they should want to play, especially if you bring an enticing toy along.

Ask if the kitten has been exposed to "scary" noises like barking dogs or vacuum cleaners. Has the kitten been introduced to traveling in a cat carrier? Did it show any special level of anxiety at the vet clinic? Can the breeder provide references from previous successful adoptions? Can you speak to those people?

Don't forget to find out about the various types of guarantees that should be part of any adoption agreement.

Primarily there should be a guarantee

of good health, and a requirement that the kitten see a vet within 72 hours to prove that is the case. (Many catteries require presentation of a receipt from this visit.)

Never let any existing cats in the household have contact with a new kitten until a vet has checked the baby's health. Many infectious feline diseases can be transferred by something as simple as a nose tap.

How to Tell if a Bengal Kitten is Healthy

Kittens should have good muscle tone, with clean coats. At about six weeks of age, Bengal kittens develop the "fuzzies," a kind of dull camouflage coat that protects them from predators as they grow.

By the time you are meeting the kittens, they should be at least 3 months old, and the fuzzies should be lessening. At eight months, the protective baby fur will be gone altogether, and the rosette pattern will be fully visible.

The fur should be very soft and silky, with no thin spots. Gently blow on the fur to part the hairs. There should be no dry or flaky skin present.
The kitten's eyes should be brightly alert, with no discharge. The nose should also be clear of discharge, and there should be no sniffling or sneezing.

Look for clean, pink ears with no sign of internal debris.

Look behind the ears, on the back just above or in front of the tail, and at the base of the tail for black specks of "flea dirt." If parasites are present, they are most detectable in these areas.

Information You Should Receive from the Breeder

In addition to the adoption contract and receipt for payment, a breeder should provide to you:

- Documentation of any and all vaccines with a schedule of when the next injections are required.

- A sheet detailing the diet the kitten has received along with amounts and feeding times.

- A pedigree giving information on name, date of birth, coloration, and registration number.

How Much Does a Bengal Kitten Cost?

In the world of pedigreed cats, the distinction is between "show" quality and "pet" quality. Show quality cats not only meet the specified standard for the breed, but they are suitable to be used in breeding programs.

Pet quality cats will have some "imperfection," like a lack of good contrast in the coat colors, or perhaps overly large ears. To the layperson, however, these "problems" are negligible in the face of the Bengal's incredible beauty.

Show quality Bengals sell in the range of $1000 - $3000 US / £636.02 - £1,908.06 UK / $1,018.65 - $3,055.95 CAD. (Note that this is an approximation. Depending on bloodlines, some show quality Bengals can cost significantly more.)

Pet quality Bengals sell for $500 - $1000 US / £318 - £636.02 UK / $509.28 - $1,018.65 CAD.

Pros and Cons of Owning a Bengal

The most commonly cited pros and cons of this breed are:

Pros:

- The breed thrives on human companionship and is highly interactive and interested in its humans.

- Respond well to behavior modification from owners who understand their quirks.

- Seem to get along well with dogs as well as children that treat them with kindness.

- Extremely loyal and loving with their humans.

- Are known for their strong, engaging personalities and sense of humor.

 - Can be a good fit for an owner that can fully appreciate a cat with "dog-like" behavior traits like fetching, leash-walking, and dependency on its owner.

Cons

- When bored and lonely, Bengals can become both aggressive and destructive.

- Can be very loud vocally, and howl when lonely.

- Some can respond in an aggressive way when disciplined.

- Often create problems with spraying.

- Get carried away with climbing and exploring.

- Are predatory around birds, fowl, small rodents, and fish.

One thing is quite clear. Although Bengals are domestic cats, they are not like any other domestic cat you will have ever raised.

Be sure you know exactly what you're getting into before you welcome a Bengal into your life — for you sake, and for the cat's.

Chapter 3 - Having a Bengal in Your Life: Daily Care

It might be more accurate to say that you need to prepare to be taken care of by a Bengal rather than the other way around. Although they need a lot of care and attention from you, their basic needs are not all that different from any other cat breed.

Have all the Necessary Supplies on Hand

When you're bringing a Bengal kitten home, be sure to talk to your breeder and find out the things to which the kitten has become accustomed:

- Use the same type of litter box with the same type of litter.
- Get the same kind of food and water bowls.
- Buy the food (wet and dry) currently being eaten.

Also ask the breeder for a recommendation about age-appropriate wet and dry foods moving forward.

Bengals and Litter Box Issues

It is not true that Bengals, as a breed, have more problems with inappropriate litter box use than any other kind of cat. Any shelter will tell you that the number one reason cited for a cat being given up is "going" outside the box.

In the vast majority of cases, the issue lies more with the human than the cat, however, the first thing you must do if a cat goes "off" its box is to have the cat examined for a urinary tract infection. In the cat's mind, if it hurts to go "in there," the logical thing is to get outside of that painful place.

A change of environment like moving to a new home or traveling in a vehicle may also trigger accidents due to stress, but this is usually temporary.

However, since cats are highly territorial — and Bengals more so — once a cat does start to go outside the box, it's hard to get them back on track. They will go where they think they are supposed to go, and that's usually the place they've "marked."

You want the cat to clearly identify the box as "the" place to go. To that end, do your job and scoop the box every day! Cats are fastidiously clean animals and they do not like a nasty box. If you wouldn't use it, they probably don't like it either.

Also, cats have definite preferences about type of box and texture of litter. Some cats don't like to be watched, and far prefer a covered box. Others prefer sand over gravel, and will completely reject any of the environmentally friendly compressed pellet litters made of various plant fibers or even newspaper.

Don't switch things up on the cat. If your cat has always used the box faithfully, and you change the type of box, from covered to pan, and suddenly the cat is "missing," it doesn't take a lot to figure out why. The cat doesn't like the box.

Be consistent, both in terms of maintenance and product use, and your Bengal should be just as good about the litter box as any other type of cat.

Bengals and Water Bowls

You can pretty well resign yourself to your Bengal playing in its water. This is especially true if you're using a recirculating water bowl, which is accepted as one of the best ways to get cat to drink more water.

The choice is up to you, but on a whole, Bengals are good drinkers, and the real issue will be mopping up the mess when he happily splashes in his bowl.

Get a Serious Scratching Post

Bengals are not cats that just lay around and stare out the window. This is an active and vigorous breed. When they scratch, they *scratch*. Providing a Bengal kitten with a serious scratching post early in life is the best way to get them not to tear up your furniture, weather stripping and rugs.

Prices on scratching equipment varies widely. It's possible to get an absolute indoor playground, which is a good idea for a cat as active as a Bengal.

The traditional, small "pole" model covered in carpet generally sells for as little as $20-$30 / £12.74-£19.11 UK / $20.39-$30.58 CAD while an elaborate "tree" outfitted with stairs, ramps, perches, and hiding areas might sell for $100 US (£65 UK / $101.95 CAD) to $300 US (£196.96 UK / $305.85 CAD) or even more.

If your Bengal does start scratching in forbidden places, consider using herbal deterrents like pennyroyal or orange essence. Cats dislike both scents. The products retail for $12-$15 US / £7.87-£9.84 UK / $12.23 - $15.29 CAD.

Double-sided tape products can also be good. Cats don't like things that feel tacky on their paws. Note that you may need a lot of this stuff, however, and this approach can get pricey. Expect to pay $8-$10 US / £5.25-$6.56 UK / $8.15 - $10.19 CAD).

Bengal Proof the House

Kittens are, by nature, little maniacs, and *Bengal* kittens are worse. They don't have the ability to judge a good idea from a bad one, just the intelligence, curiosity, and drive to go for what they want to try.

Get anything out of the house that your Bengal might get tangled up in, like the cords on all that enticing electronic stuff. Tape the wires to the baseboard, or encase them in cord minder products.

It's also a good idea to cap open electrical outlets. Also be aware of anything that might be a choke and swallow hazard.

Relocate or secure heavy objects, or really anything big that might get tipped over or pulled down. With Bengals, it's a really good idea to secure all cabinet doors with baby latches, especially if toxic items are stored inside, including household cleaning agents.

Indoor vs. Outdoor Controversy

The dominant reason why Bengals should be indoor cats is their exotic appearance. Certainly they are well suited as predators to survive outside, but they can easily be mistaken for a wild animal and be killed.

They also have a tendency to be dominant and aggressive with other animals on their "territory", behavior which can also be mistaken as "wild" rather than as a personality quirk of the breed.

It should also be noted that because Bengals are exceptionally skilled climbers and jumpers, it can be difficult to get them down from trees once they've had a taste of the outdoors.

Leash Training

The real upside is that Bengals are one of the most adaptable of all breeds to leash training if you start them young. Older animals are more difficult to train.

Outfitted with a secure harness and lead, and given access to trees, a Bengal will happily and safely explore outdoors. In truth, given the overall Bengal personality, they are more likely to think they're the ones leading *you* on the leash.

Food and Water

Bengals are domestic cats, and they should be fed as domestic cats, however, you always want to find a high-quality food that meets all their needs, in particular their protein requirement, which biologically is quite high.

No cat can survive on a vegetarian diet. These animals need 50 percent more protein per pound of body weight than dogs and humans.

Additionally, they require fats, but not carbohydrates, which is why so many retail grade cat foods really aren't all that good for your pet. Look at the label. They're packed with plant-based carbohydrates that fill the cat up, but don't give it the nutrition it needs.

Basically, the less you pay for cat food, the more likely it is to be overly dense in plant-based fillers.

Because Bengals are often described as having "dog like" characteristics, some owners mistakenly think they can be fed dog food. This is not the case. Dog food does not have enough fat and protein for a cat, nor does it contain an amino acid that is key to feline health — taurine.

Give your Bengal fresh, clean water at all times. Water is essential for all the animal's physical processes, and, while many cats are not big water drinkers, this is hardly an issue with a Bengal. In fact, you can't keep them out of the water!

With a Bengal in the house, the floor space around his bowl will be the cleanest in the house because you'll be constantly mopping up after his splashing!

If you really want to give a Bengal a treat, get him a water dish with a circulating fountain for about $30 US(£19.70 UK / $30.57 CAD).He'll not only drink out of it, he'll think it's the best cat toy EVER!

Grooming

Bengals are not high-maintenance cats due to their tight, short pelt, which lies close to the skin. Their fur is dense and semi-waterproof, which explains in part the breed's great love for playing in the water — it simply rolls off their backs.

Bathing a Bengal is no trick at all since many will just walk right in the shower with you. Some individuals like water more than others, but all Bengals play in water to some extent, as evidence by the splashed mess they so often leave around their water bowls.

The truly important chore with a Bengal is to keep their claws well-trimmed. They are vigorous scratchers, and need their own scratching "post" — bigger is better with a Bengal. Declawing is so universally decried as inhumane that it is even outlawed in some regions.

If you get your Bengal accustomed to having its claws clipped, this should not be an issue. Be prepared, however to keep up with the chore on a weekly basis, or see the shredded results around the house.

Monthly and Annual Costs

In terms of their regular care and dietary needs, Bengals are no more expensive than any short-haired breed. The approximate lifetime costs for a pet quality Bengal based on an average lifespan of 12-16 years is:

- \$18,780 to \$25,040 US
- £12,336 to £16,448 UK

- $19,130 to $25,507 CAD

Those calculations are based on a projected annual cost of:

- $1,565 US
- £1,028 UK
- $1,594 CAD

Per month, that breaks down to:

- $130 US
- £85.40 UK
- $132.44 CAD

Bear in mind that the costs for show cats will be much higher based on multiple factors included, but not limited to:

- grooming,
- show entry fees,
- travel, lodging,
- membership and registration fees.

Overall, Bengals are very healthy cats, so vet bills should be along the lines of normal procedures like spaying / neutering, vaccinations, dental care, and annual exams. See Chapter 4 - Bengal Healthcare for more information.

Chapter 4 - Bengal Healthcare

Overall, Bengals are extremely healthy cats. Like all domestic cats, however, they need to start their lives with the correct veterinarian care. Preventive care on your part and regular checkups will ensure that you have your devoted companion for the full span of its life.

(Note that it is a mistaken notion that it is difficult to get a vet to treat a Bengal because the cat is in any way "wild" or "unusual" in its physiology.

Bengals are fully domesticated cats and can be treated by any competent small animal veterinarian.)

Spaying and Neutering

Consult with both the breeder and your veterinarian on the timing of these procedures, which are normally required for pet quality Bengal adoptions.

It is standard procedure for kittens to be spayed or neutered at roughly eight months of age. Do not be surprised if the terms of your adoption contract require you to present proof that you have honored this clause of the agreement.

Regardless, these procedures should be performed on either a male or female Bengal kitten before they reach six months of age.

Vet clinics charge across a fairly broad range for their services. It is possible to have a kitten spayed or neutered for around $50 US (£32.82 UK / $51.08 CAD).

The truly important thing, however, is that you choose a good veterinarian who works in safe conditions. Discuss all possible complications, including the use of anesthesia before agreeing to go forward with the procedure.

Bengals are highly sensitive to anesthesia and can suffer from allergic reactions that result in coronary arrest.

Also, stop and consider that having your Bengal spayed or neutered might be the point at which you establish a long-term relationship with a vet.

Rather than thinking about saving money, this might be when you want to consider choosing a vet who will care for your cat throughout his life.

Taking the time to interview prospective vets, and perhaps spending a little more in the beginning, might offer much larger returns in the long run for both you and your cat.

Vaccinations

To some extent, in both cats and humans, vaccinations have become a point of controversy. Certainly the use of vaccinations in companion animals has reduced the spread of infectious disease.

As mentioned earlier, this is particularly true in cats, where many such diseases are spread just a nose "tap."

It is true that there have been cases of tumors in cats developing at the site the shots were administered. This is something you can discuss with both your breeder and with the vet before arriving at a decision.

If you move forward, the typical regimen of vaccinations and the intervals at which they are given follow this course:

- At six weeks, the distemper combo*, with a second shot every 3-4 weeks until 16 months of age. After a booster at one year, the vaccine is re-administered on a three year schedule.

- At eight weeks, feline leukemia with a repeat inoculation in 3-4 weeks, thereafter followed by an annual booster.

- Rabies, administered according to local regulations and repeated annually as per the applicable law.

* This vaccine combines antibodies for panleukopenia (FPV or feline infectious enteritis), rhinotracheitis (FVR is an upper respiratory or pulmonary infection), and calicivirus (causes respiratory infections). It may also include protection from Chlamydophilia (causes conjunctivitis).

Expect to pay a minimum price of $40 US (£26.26 UK / $40.86 CAD) per individual shot. (Again, prices vary widely by veterinarian practice.)

Preventative Healthcare

In recent years, veterinarians, working with owners, have furthered the cause of preventive health care in all companion animals by a simple process of education. Knowing how to monitor your cat's behavior for signs of illness will not only keep your beloved pet happy and well, but it will reduce the potential costs of reactive veterinary visits.

How to Recognize Warning Signs In Your Cat

The best way to spot signs of ill health in a cat is to be intimately familiar with the animal's normal behavior. Bengals actually make this quite easy because they are so highly interactive and have such a desire to be present in their human's lives.

Petting and playing with the cat allows you a perfect opportunity to judge its overall condition and to look for such things as:

- Weight changes. This extends to both gains and losses. Bengals are sleek, muscular animals. They should have a healthy pad of fat covering their rib cage, but you should be able to feel the ribs when you press lightly.

- Changes in movement. Bengals are highly agile, athletic animals. Any reluctance to jump, any sign of limping, or any loss of ability to perform "normal" tasks should be evaluated. Cats can injure themselves, but it is in their nature to hide their pain as an aspect of self-preservation.

- Changes in the condition of the nose. A cat's nose should always be moist, with no signs of cracking or bleeding. Additionally, the nose and the area around it should be clean, and free of staining or discharge.

- An unusual expression or condition of the eyes. Bengals have bright, alert eyes. Their pupils should be of equal size and centered. The eyes should be moist, with no discoloration of the whites and few blood vessels visible. If the cat has watering or discharge from the eyes, it should be evaluated for an upper respiratory infection of even allergies.

- Dirty or smelly ears. Your cat's ears should be dry, perfectly smooth, and completely free of irritation. Persistent scratching of the ears, a build-up of debris, and a yeasty odor indicate the presence of parasitic mites. Any time a cat flinches when its ears are touched, a trip to the vet is in order.

- Dirty teeth or discolored gums. A cat's teeth should be white, and the gums should be pink and healthy with no lumps or bumps. All cats are susceptible to oral cancers, so monitoring dental and oral health is essential.

- Poor capillary refill time. Gently press against the cat's gums. The spot should go white, and then rapidly become pink again. If the refill time is more than a second or two, the cat's circulatory system might not be functioning properly.

Although some cat owners balk at the idea, brushing your cat's teeth is a crucial aspect of preventive healthcare. If you start the animal at a young age, it's usually possible to get them to submit to this process.

It is rare for a cat to submit to having its teeth cleaned at the vet's without anesthesia, although some practices purport to attempt the procedure.

Given the sensitivity of the Bengal breed to anesthesia, owners are well served to train a cat to have its teeth brushed as early in life as possible so that only annual dental exams are required.

Feline tooth brushes and tooth paste can be purchased from your vet or in most retail pet stores at a cost of $7-$10 US (£4.60-£6.56 UK / $7.15-$10.21 CAD).

In addition to these warning signs, pay attention to how your cat breathes. Cats breathe primarily from the chest. The abdomen should barely move on inhalation and exhalation.

On a regular basis, run your hands over the cat's entire body. (Your Bengal will love this "examination.") Any bump or growth should be evaluated by your vet immediately.

Dehydration is rarely a problem with Bengals since they love water so much. A way to test that your cat is getting enough water is to "tent" the skin between the shoulder blades. Simply pull the skin up and release it quickly. The skin should go right back in place. If it does not, and if the animal's gums seem dry to the touch, dehydration might be present.

Behavior is a Key Indicator of Health

Remember, as a survival instinct, cats hide signs of pain and illness. Watch for others signs of distress or discomfort. While Bengals do have a reputation for developing litter box avoidance issues, never assume this is just a breed trait.

If there is an "incident," have the cat checked for a urinary infection. Often if a cat tries to "go" in the box and experiences pain, there instinct is to get away from the place where they were hurt. Undetected urinary tract infections are often the cause of going outside the box.

Bladder blockages are also a danger in neutered males, and changes in litter box habits can also signal the onset of diabetes.

Common Illnesses and Conditions in Bengal Cats

Although Bengals are healthy cats, there are a number of conditions that can manifest in the breed.

Retinal Atrophy and Cataracts

Retinal atrophy, the deterioration of the rods and cones in the retina leading to blindness, is common in this breed. There is no way to screen for the carrier gene, and carriers themselves may be immune.

Consequently, even young cats are susceptible to the condition, and breeders will not cover retinal atrophy in their health guarantees.

Bengals are susceptible to developing cataracts, but these can be surgically removed. Again, however, it is best to avoid surgery whenever possible with a Bengal because they are prone to allergic reactions to anesthesia that can result in life-threatening cardiac arrest.

> *Note that not all vets are aware of the issue of Bengals and anesthesia. You may need to be prepared to educate your vet!*

Joint Problems

Since Bengals are so active, they can experience a painful dislocation of the knee joint called patellar luxation. This can also be a genetic malformation present from birth. The only remedy is surgery, which again raises the issue of anesthesia.

One of the best ways to protect your cat from this problem is to make sure his weight remains at a normal level. Overweight cats experience much greater strain on their joints.

Heart Disease

Bengals, especially older cats, can be subject to developing hypertrophic cardiomyopathy (HCM), which is a thickening of the heart muscle causing it to work harder.

This can lead to blood clots, which may cause a total loss of the use of the animal's hind legs, or to congestive heart failure resulting in death.

Early signs of the condition include early signs include panting and lethargy. A sonogram is used to test for the presence of HCM at a cost of $250-$400 US / £127-£255 UK / $204-$408 CAD.

Feline Leukemia

Although the Bengal breed originated in part from research being conducted into feline leukemia immunity in Asian Leopard Cats, Bengals themselves are *not* immune to feline leukemia.

Pet-quality Bengals have only 12.5% "wild" blood. This is not sufficient to afford them even partial immunity to this devastating and highly contagious disease.

Loose Stools

Bengals can exhibit loose stools even when they test negative for intestinal parasites like Giardiasis, Coccidiosis, and Tritrichomonas.

Many veterinarians suspect that food allergies underly this issue, which can often be resolved by feeding the cat a higher fiber, "hairball" dry food, making sure they have adequate taurine, and supplementing their diet with raw food.

*(**Note**: Never feed you cat a "raw" diet without first investigating exactly what is entailed to ensure that all the animal's nutritional needs are being met. Raw diets are controversial for both dogs and cats, but many pet owners swear by the process. Conduct thorough research before radically altering your pet's diet.)*

Upper Respiratory Problems

All catteries battle issue with upper respiratory infections (URI). The only real treatment for cats that have contracted a URI virus is isolation. The most common signs are running eyes and sneezing.

The virus is airborne and will spread quickly. L-Lysine supplementation is usually sufficient to resolve the problem, but it should not be ignored.

Hypoallergenic

Although this is more a health issue for humans than for the Bengal, most breeders are in agreement that while the cats are not completely hypoallergenic, they are better tolerated by allergy sufferers.

This is likely a consequence of the breed's short, dense pelt and lower production of the protein Fel d 1 present in a cat's saliva and sebaceous glands.

Chapter 5 - Breeding Bengals

There are many things to evaluate before starting a breeding program with any kind of cat, but Bengals are NOT ordinary cats.

If one Bengal requires high levels of interaction and attention from its humans, running a Bengal cattery is like opening a boarding school for highly intelligent, super needy feline geniuses.

Things to Consider Before Becoming a Breeder

First, do not think that breeding cats will make you rich. It won't. Even the most highly successful breeders admit that in a good year they break even.

Certainly you will make money when you sell a kitten, which you will promptly use to pay your tab at the vet clinic, top off the food supply, and get those new scratching posts your Bengals have been demanding.

Money flows out of a cattery as fast as it comes in. All breeders go through this situation — ask them!

Talk to Other Breeders

Part of your decision-making process in becoming a breeder should be talking to other breeders.

You need to meet and learn from people who are working with the kind of cat in which you are interested and who will candidly tell you exactly what lies ahead — the good and the bad.

There are many venues open to you to explore breeding Bengals:

- Attend a cat show and collect business cards.

Don't try to get into a lengthy discussion with a Bengal breeder at a cat show. If you've never attended one of these events, they are amazingly chaotic.

Exhibitors have very little time to get the show ring, and they're preoccupied with the business at hand. Just get contact information from people in your area or whose cats you find exceptionally beautiful.

- Join a local or regional breed club.

The best place to start is the home page of The International Bengal Cat Society (TIBCS) at www.BengalCat.com.

- Learn as much as you can about the Bengal breed.

The TIBCS publishes a bulletin and Bengals Illustrated at www.BengalsIllustrated.com is an excellent resource.

- Join breeder discussion forums.

The Internet has made it possible for cat enthusiasts all over the world to connect and discuss the animals they love.

Use your favorite search engine to find either breed specific or general feline discussion forums that talk about becoming a cat breeder.

A Word on Forum Etiquette

If you've never participated in an online discussion forum, there will be a specific area of the community where you can introduce yourself. In the beginning, you will want to read more than "talk."

Get to know the rules of the community and the personalities involved. When you are conducting discussions by writing only, thought and tone can be easily misconstrued. Learn the ropes first. Don't just jump in.)

The bottom line on becoming a cat breeder is *not* money. It's love of the breed and a desire to improve its genetic quality. Don't go into this hobby — and it is a hobby, not a profession — unless you have that level of commitment.

Ask Yourself the Tough Questions

It's imperative that you ask yourself some tough and important questions. Be very honest with yourself about the answers.

- Are you willing to sacrifice the time that is required every day, including holidays, to give your Bengals the attention, care, and love they need and deserve?

- Do you have the financial resources to meet all the physical, mechanical, and logistical needs of a cattery and are you prepared to lose money on this project?

- Do you have the room, or can you acquire the room to adequately house (in clean and well-kept conditions), a highly active and social breed like the Bengal? Are you prepared to even remodel your home if the need should arise?

- Are you in a sufficiently isolated location, have the ability to soundproof your home, or have good relations with your neighbors? One Bengal is loud enough. Imagine a breeding pair (or pairs) and their offspring forming a yowling feline chorus as the mood strikes them.

- Is your family supportive of the endeavor and do they realize the amount of time and financial resources you will be dedicating to this project? Are they willing to help if they are needed?

- If you do not have a family, can you afford to hire help or do you have a support system in place in case you are ill or have to be away? And are those people willing to get to know your Bengals in advance?

- Are you prepared to stay up hand-rearing kittens in the event that one of your queens rejects her litter?

- Can you handle the emotionally wrenching heartbreak of watching sickly kittens die?

- Are you prepared for the even more emotionally wrenching experience of having the kittens you have loved and to whom you have become attached go to new homes?

Be warned, if you love cats, you'll want to keep every one of those kittens! For the vast majority of people, that's just not practical — especially with a breed like the Bengal.

Explore All the Reasons NOT to Be a Breeder

Breeding cats is not for everyone, and there are some very good reasons NOT to do it. You need to think about those as well, and ask yourself if you are falling prey to the many myths that abound about cats and litters.

- Your cat will not "miss" or "mourn" if she does not have a litter of her own.

Yes, many cats are very good mothers, including Bengals, but that doesn't mean they won't live perfectly happy fulfilled lives as single "career" gals.

- A cat does not "need" to have a litter before being neutered.

Young female cats should be spayed before six months of age. There is actually a greater chance of medical complication in a cat that young *giving* birth than in *notgiving* birth.

- Your children do not "need" the experience of raising a litter of kittens, especially highly specialized cats like Bengals.

That is not to imply that children shouldn't be exposed to the cycle of life or taught to gently respect and care for young animals.

There are, however, many ways to give your children that experience without taking on the responsibility of caring for a litter of kittens that will grow up into active and demanding cats.

Also, you cannot ignore the fact that your children may become very attached to the kittens, making it all the more difficult to give the cats up for adoption.

Breeding Cats At This Level is Not a "Project"

Breeding cats is a way of life, not a one-time project to be taken up lightly, completed and then put aside. It requires a huge financial commitment, and joining a "culture" of breed clubs and associated organizations with membership fees and breed standards.

If you want to raise registered Bengals, your Bengals must be registered. You must have a fair understanding of genetics, and a commitment to the highest quality dietary considerations and level of veterinary care.
And there will be costs. More costs than you can even imagine in the beginning.

The Cost of Breeding Bengals

If you decide to become a cat breeder, you will have all the regular expenses associated with cat care times the number of cats you own.

Add to those a huge range of ancillary expenses including, but certainly not limited to:

- reference books and materials $75-$150 US (£48-£197 UK / $79-$158 CAD)

- a quality breeding queen $1750-$2500 US (£1135-£1621 UK / $1840-$2628 CAD)

- a quality breeding stud $3000+ US (£1946+ UK / $3154 CAD)

- stud fees $500-$1000 US (£324-£648 UK / $525-$1051 CAD)

- repeat FIV/FELV tests for males and females prior to mating visits $25-$100 US (£16-£64 UK / $26-$105 CAD)

- routine veterinary care including, but not limited to regular check-ups, blood work, and heart scans $700-$800 US (£453-£518 UK / $736-$841 CAD) per cat per year

- kittening pens $100-$250 US (£64-£197 UK / $105-$263 CAD)

- additional cat furniture and toys $175-$350 US (£113-£226 UK / $184-$368 CAD)

- emergency vet services during pregnancies, $175 US (£113 UK) for the visit and $1200+ US (£778+ UK / $818 CAD) for a C-section

Also remember that you will be keeping intact cats. If you have a breeding pair, you will have to keep them separated to prevent unplanned litters, which can double your costs for basic housing set-up in terms of equipment and diversions.

"Aren't You Being a Downer?"

Yes, absolutely, because no one should make a snap decision to become a cat breeder. If, however, you've considered all these factors, learned as much as you can about the breed, talked with people who are doing what you want to do, gotten the support of your family and friends — and still want to be a Bengal breeder?

You're in for the adventure of a lifetime.

The joys and rewards of making your life with one Bengal are legion. Living in a community of these gorgeous cats, and actively working to improve the breed is an endeavor that will give you hours of pure pleasure and real pride in your animals.

And yes, you won't be able to give them all up. There will always be that one kitten in the litter who wins your heart. You will wind up being the "crazy cat lady" or "crazy cat guy," but for one simple and over-riding reason. It's almost impossible not to be crazy about a Bengal.

Afterword

The development of the Bengal breed was a labor of love among a dedicated group of cat enthusiasts who envisioned a small, beautiful cat with a wild appearance, but a gentle and devoted personality. The reality of the Bengal far exceeds the dream of its creators.

Over the past 20 years, Bengals have grown in popularity as devoted companions, even exceeding the fame of the Siamese for their interactive personalities, loyal devotion to their humans, and remarkable vocal abilities.

Bengals are talkers and thinkers. They cannot imagine being anywhere but with you, and they're certainly not going to keep their opinions to themselves!

Keen observers and clever mimics, Bengals watch the world around them and in particular, their favorite part of the world — you. They not only learn, but they extrapolate, exhibiting complicated thought patterns and an almost uncanny ability to problem solve.

With their love of splashing water, and their acrobatic climbing abilities, these are active, engaged, involved cats, not couch potatoes. Bengals adapt extremely well to harness and leash because there's just so much out there to see and do.

Many Bengal owners feel that their cats are "walking" them, and not the other way around.

Make no mistake, owning a Bengal is a huge commitment. These cats have an emotional need for their people. They cannot be left alone for long periods of time, and they are perfectly capable of being absolute little demons when they're bored or annoyed with you.

These are not, however "wild" cats. The Bengal is a gentle, intelligent, responsive, and fully domesticated house pet.

They are not just beautiful for their golden coats and vivid stripes and rosettes. A Bengal is just as beautiful inside, blessed with a delightful, loving, and inquisitive disposition.

Be forewarned. A Bengal may well ruin you for any other breed. By turns demanding and even annoying, they are also beguiling and rewarding for the right owners.

If you want a cat that will sit in the window or lie quietly on the rug, the Bengal is not the pet for you. But if you want a friend, a companion, and a confidante, there is no better choice than the Bengal.

Relevant Websites

Bengals Illustrated
http://www.bengalsillustrated.com/home

The International Bengal Cat Society, Inc.
http://www.tibcs.com/breeders.pdf
and
http://www.bengalcat.com/aboutbengals/bengal.php

Wikipedia Information
http://en.wikipedia.org/wiki/Bengal_(cat)

Blog on Bengal Cats
http://www.bengalcats.co/

VetStreet – Articles and Information written by Veterinarians
http://www.vetstreet.com/cats/bengal

Petfinder - Breed Information
http://www.petfinder.com/cat-breeds/Bengal

Absolutely Bengals
http://www.absolutelybengals.com/pages/bengalhist.html

Catster – Breed Information
http://www.catster.com/cat-breeds/Bengal

Titan Bengals – Bengals for sale as well as great breed info.
http://www.titanbengals.com/bengal-kittens-questions-answers.php

Cats of Australia – Australian Breed Information site.
http://www.catsofaustralia.com/bengal-cat-description.htm

Mystre Bengals – Cattery near Houston TX
http://www.mystre.com/

Bengal Classifieds
http://www.bengalclassifieds.com/bengal-cat-education-history.htm

Eriador Cats – Bengal Breed Information
http://www.eriador-cats.com/ec/ec_bengal_genetics.php

Bengal Cat – UK site
http://www.bengalcat.co.uk/

Animal World – Bengal Breed Information
http://cats.animal-world.com/Hybrid-Cats/BengalCat.php

Videos

http://animal.discovery.com/tv-shows/cats-101/videos/bengal.htm

https://www.youtube.com/watch?v=F_oQALXNnPg

http://www.tica.org/members/publications/std_rules.pdf?zoom_highlight=cheetoh#search=%22cheetoh%22

Legislation and the Bengal Cat
http://www.bengalcat.com/Flier.pdf

Frequently Asked Questions

What exactly is a "Bengal" cat?

The Bengal is a breed developed by crossing a domestic house cat with an Asian Leopard Cat.

Are Bengal cats expensive?

All breeders classify their kittens as either "show" quality or "pet" quality. Show quality cats conform to established breed standards and are suitable to compete and to participate in breeding programs. Pet quality Bengals have some perceived imperfection that deviates from that standard.

Prices are set accordingly with show quality Bengals selling in the range of:

- $1000 - $3000 US
- £636.02 - £1,908.06 UK
- $1,018.65 - $3,055.95 CAD

Pet quality Bengals sell for:

$500 - $1000 US
£318 - £636.02 UK
$509.28 - $1,018.65 CAD.

I don't understand terms like "filial," "F1," and "SBT." Are they important in understanding the Bengal I buy?

Those terms are extremely important. The dictionary definition of *filial* is "of or relating to a generation or the sequence of generations following the parental generation."

So, if a breeder says a cat is an F1, the kitten is a first generation cross between an Asian Leopard Cat and a domestic Bengal.

An F2 is a cross between an F1 and a domestic Bengal, so that cat has an ALC grandparent.

An F3 is the offspring of an F2 and a Bengal, so the cat has an ALC great-grandparent.

An F4 is considered to be a SBT (studbook tradition) Bengal by the International Cat Association (TICA), making the cat eligible for competition.

An F4 or SBT Bengal is a fully accepted domestic cat or a "domestic Bengal," with an ALC great-great-grandparent.

What is an Asian Leopard Cat?

The Asian Leopard Cat is a small, wild spotted cat that was used to create the hybrid Bengal cat breed. Asian Leopard Cats or ALCs average about 10 pounds (4 kg) in weight.

How active are Bengals?

Very. You'll never find a Bengal just hanging out, lolling on the sofa, content to sleep most of the day. Bengals need to be able to climb. They love toys and cat trees, and most of all, interaction with you.

How much do Bengals climb?

A lot! These cats are thorough investigators. They'll check out everything at ground level, and then start going up, and up, and up. If you have breakable decorative items, get them put away in a cabinet or breakage will ensue.

When a domestic cat has checked out an area once or twice, they tend to leave it alone. Bengals will go back, time after time after time.

Are Bengal cats large?

Bengals vary in size in relation to the genetics of their pedigree line, but on average, you can expect the mails to weigh 12-15 pounds (5-6 kg), with females at 8-12 pounds (3-5 kg). Body length should be 22" or greater (roughly 56 cm).

How much attention does a Bengal really need?

Many people get a cat because it requires less attention than a dog. That is NOT the case with a Bengal. They need as much or *more* attention than a dog. Your Bengal will be devoted to you, but you must be devoted to him.

Let a Bengal get bored and be prepared for the consequences. Left to their own devices, these cats are beyond creative in what they can get into.

I've heard Bengals have litter box issues. Is that true?

It is true that some Bengals go "off" their boxes. All cats are extremely particular about their boxes. When you've ruled out a medical problem like a urinary tract infection, a cat urinating or eliminating outside the box may be objecting to the condition of the box, the texture of the litter, or even the shape of the box. Once a cat has started going outside, it is hard to get them back on track, but not impossible.

It's best, from the very start, to replicate exactly the type of box and litter the kitten used from the beginning and never to diverge from that pattern. Many breeders contend that Bengals like softer, finer litter that feels more like sand under their paws.

What does a Bengal's coat feel like?

Silk. Their fur is absolutely lovely, really more like a pelt, that is not only visually beautiful, but luxurious to the touch.

What is a Bengal's temperament like?

These cats are truly kind, sweet, and gentle. Many exhibit a whimsical sense of humor, and their devotion to their humans is absolute. Like any animal, if treated poorly, a Bengal will react accordingly.

If, however, these beautiful cats get the care, love, and attention they want and deserve, they are wonderful companions and friends. There are literally no other cats like them.

Are Bengal cats good with children?

Bengals make very good family pets and love to play with kids, and generally to sleep with them. The important thing is to teach your children how to behave appropriately toward *all* animals. Kindness begets kindness. Any animal of any species may get testy with children who are, no matter how unwittingly, unkind to them.

How much do Bengals shed?

Bengals do shed, but very little. It might take as long as a month for a Bengal to deposit as much hair on the sofa as a domestic cat could lay down in a week.

There are occasions when a Bengal will begin to shed heavily for no apparently reason. This can be due to stress or a change in the weather. Daily doses of a good vet-quality Omega-3 fatty acid will generally stop the problem.

How would you describe the Bengal's color and patterning?

A Bengal's spots are aligned horizontally, not randomly or in the traditional "tabby" pattern. The important thing for show quality Bengals is that the spots contrast sharply against the background color.

All pattern edges must be distinct and sharp. Spots can be tan, brown, cinnamon, chocolate, or black, with spots also occurring on the belly.

What do Bengal cats eat?

Cats need high-quality wet and dry food. All cats are carnivores, and they have high protein requirements. Additionally, cats gain less weight on wet food. Bengals are slender, muscular cats.

Feed your cat the highest quality foods you can afford, and begin by consulting with your breeder and matching or exceeding the type of food your Bengal received in the cattery.

Can I leash train my Bengal?

Not only do Bengals take well to leash training, but they will instantly learn how to successfully climb trees right to the point the leash will stop them.

A walk with its human is the highlight of a Bengal's day, and they're even happier if you take along a dangling toy on a wand and engineer a vigorous round of acrobatics on the lawn.

When I shop for toys for my Bengal, what should I buy?

Bengals like the same sorts of toys as most cats, but go for the industrial strength models. Bengals are strong, so the better quality toys will bear up under the abuse better.

I read something about glitter and Bengals. What's that about?

Bengal glitter is an aspect of the animal's coat derived from a recessive gene gained through the wild Egyptian Mau. It gives the coat a metallic appearance that literally glitters in the sunlight. This look does not occur in all Bengals, but when it does, it's spectacular.

How do Bengal cats sound?

Bengals are highly vocal cats with a wide vocal repertoire. They can, by turns yowl, growl, squeak, giggle, scream, and even emit a perfectly normal meow. Sometimes the transition from one sound to another is accompanied by a gurgle of sorts.

Do Bengals suffer from separation anxiety?

You can only leave a Bengal alone for a short period of time. Frequent travelers and people who work long hours are not good candidates to own a Bengal.

It cannot be emphasized enough that Bengals need more and more attention. They will work themselves into every aspect of your life. If they are left alone and start feeling abandoned, they'll act out, destroying items and often eliminating inappropriately.

Will Bengals transfer their affections from one person to another?

Obviously Bengals that are given up for rescue will have to learn to adapt to new people, but when Bengals pick "their" person, that bond is indestructible.
It's very hard for a Bengal to be separated from their human, and if that person dies, the cat will grieve inconsolably — some to the point of dying as well.

How clean are Bengals in their habits?

The only word for a Bengal is fastidious. They get almost obsessed with cleaning themselves to the point that they literally smell clean.

Are Bengal cats safe outdoors?

With supervision, wearing a good harness, and leashed, Bengals love to be outside, and benefit from the sunshine, fresh air and exercise. On their own, the chances that these exotic beauties might be stolen, or worse yet harmed because they look "wild" is just too great.

Should I get a Bengal?

Only get a Bengal if you also know what you're getting yourself into. These cats need attention. They need to climb. They don't like to be alone. They're loud talkers. They splash water all over the place. They're smart and born mimics.

A Bengal is quite capable of watching you flip a light switch and then recreating the action. Once they've learned something, they have it down for life.

This can translate to repeated toiled flushes, every light in the house being on, and your computer in total disarray if you've been silly enough to leave it on.

Should I get an adult "rescue" Bengal or a kitten?

If possible, especially if it's your first Bengal, a kitten is your best option, although you'll spend more money on the initial purchase. Experienced Bengal owners are excellent candidates to take in rescue Bengals because they will be more able to understand the quirks of the breed that may have led to the cat being given up in the first place.

Appendix I - History and Development of the Bengal Breed

In July 1871, the first officially sanctioned cat fanciers' event was held at The Crystal Palace in London. Many "predictable" breeds were present: Persian, Abyssinian, Manx, and Siamese, for instance.

But, there were also wild and hybrid species on display, illustrating that even at this early stage of the modern cat fancy phenomenon, small exotic cats were attracting a following.

In 1875 at a cat show in Edinburgh, Scotland an Ocelot won the "Wild or Hybrid Between Wild and Domestic Cat Class." The hybrids on display were mainly crosses of domestics with Scottish Wildcats (*felissilvestrisgrampia*) or with Caffree Cats from Egypt.

These animals are among the 30 species of wild cats in the world that are considered to be of a size comparable to domestic cats. (The big cat species are tiger, lion, jaguar, leopard, snow leopard, mountain lion, and cheetah.)

The first mention of a cross between an Asian Leopard Cat (ALC) — the progenitor of the Bengal— and a domestic cat, was in 1889 in Harrison Weir's book, *Our Cats and All About Them*. There was a reputed confirmed cross in 1934, and another in 1941, which was mentioned in a Japanese cat publication.

The Asian Leopard Cat is a small spotted wild cat widely distributed throughout Asia. Although somewhat shy, it has a history of peacefully living in proximity to humans. Depending on location, these wildcats weigh 5-12 lbs. (2.28-5.44 kg.)

Development of the Modern Bengal Breed

The real work of creating hybrid cats crossed with the ALC started in the late 1960s with Dr. Willard Centerwall. A professor of pediatrics, and of maternal and child health at the Loma Linda Medical Center, Centerwall studied feline genetics as a scientific hobby. He is credited with arriving at the definitive explanation of male calico and tortoiseshell cats.

Although Centerwall published several studies of small wild cats, his work with Asian Leopard Cats intersected research in immunocompromised individuals. That project was built on a foundation of comparative gene mapping of humans and cats. Centerwall was particularly interested in the ALC's lack of a gene for contracting feline leukemia.

The disease manifests in much the same way in people and cats, so mapping the feline genome offered rich implications for medical research into a cure for both species. Centerwall was curious if the native immunity of the ALC to leukemia could be passed on to hybrid offspring.

Where Love of the Breed and Science Meet

To conduct his tests, Centerwall only needed to collect blood from the hybrid cats. The animals then required homes. Feline enthusiast Jean Sugden Mill, had a different kind of interest in the ALC hybrids.

An opponent of the fur trade, Mill believed that if a domestic cat with a wild appearance could be cultivated and popularized, people would find it much harder to buy furs that looked like their own pets.

Mill had a long-standing interest in feline genetics going back to papers she wrote while enrolled at UC Davis in the 1940s. On her own, and working with zoo keepers in Europe, Mill produced ALC / domestic crosses in the 1960s, but none were taken past the F2 or second generation.

In 1980, Mill met Centerwall and adopted four of his hybrids, later acquiring an additional five cats. In 1982, she made a trip to India where she was introduced to a feral Indian Mau, which she incorporated into her breeding program.

Mill was not the only breeder to consider using Maus to develop a wild-looking domestic cat. In the 1980s, Greg and Elizabeth Kent used Egyptian Maus in their breeding program and were so successful that some pedigreed Bengals today still trace their origin to the Kents' cats.

The Breed Acquires a Name

Independent of this work, zoo keeper Bill Engler, a member of the Long Island Ocelot Club and the winner of the club's Lotty Award in 1967 for his devotion to exotic felines, produced two litters of cats he called "Bengals" in 1970.

His stated purpose was, "To create a small exotic cat that was beautiful and that had the disposition that was suitable for a pet house cat, that had a greater resistance to disease of civilization than his jungle-bred cousins, and that would readily reproduce himself." ("Bengal Cat Origins," http://www.bengalsillustrated.com/bengal-cat-history/#sthash.z4UCRlTx.dpuf - Accessed June 2013).

As it became more difficult to acquire and to keep small, wild cats as pets, Engler hoped the Bengal breed would fill the gap. Although Engler bred his cats to what he referred to as a "2.5" generation, no Bengal line today can be traced back to his work, although he is credited with naming the breed.

Bengal Breed Receives Recognition

Through Mill's efforts, the Bengal was recognized by The International Cat Association (TICA) in 1983. She worked tirelessly to see the breed become fully domesticated.

Mill was responsible for introducing a "domestic street cat," Millwood Toby of Delhi into her breeding program in the early 1980s. Toby had the fantastic glittered coat that is now a famous hallmark of the Bengal breed.

Mill was a tireless advocate for the breed, spending thousands of dollars to promote the cats, and traveling the world to show them. Because of her work not only in refining the Bengal's genetics, but of pulling together the efforts of so many other enthusiasts into a coordinated program to create a truly domestic cat, Mill is rightfully considered to be the true originator of the Bengal cat.

Appendix II - Filial Degree Explained

Fully domestic Bengals are removed four generations (F4) from their Asian Leopard Cat ancestor. They are "wild" in appearance only, but not in temperament.

Due to TICA judging standards disqualifying any Bengal from show that illustrates signs of aggressive behavior, the breed continues to be selectively bred for a docile, gentle nature.

An SBT (stud book tradition) Bengal is five generations or more away from an ALC ancestor. This means the cat is, at minimum, an F5.

- An F1 Bengal is the offspring of a domestic cat and an Asian Leopard Cat, and is a 50% cross.

- An F2 Bengal is the offspring of an F1 Bengal and an SBT Bengal. This creates a 25% cross.

- An F3 Bengal is the offspring of an F2 and an SBT Bengal.

In cases, F1 through F4 Bengals are still illegal due to their percentage of "wild" blood.

(For more information on regulations regarding the keeping of these cats, please see Appendix III - Bengal Cats and Legal Considerations.)

The vast majority of Bengals kept as cats today are SBTs or F5s.

Appendix III – Bengal Cats and Legal Considerations

United States

Alaska - hybrid cats are banned unless grandfathered in with a permit before 2002.

Colorado - Denver only allows Bengal F4 or lower hybrids - check your local laws for other bans.

Georgia - 4th Generation and lower Bengals allowed only.

Hawaii - All hybrids banned.

Indiana - 3rd Generation and lower allowed.

Iowa - All hybrids banned

Massachusetts - 4th Generation and lower allowed.

New Hampshire - 4th Generation and lower allowed.

New York City - No hybrids of any kind allowed at this time other than those with permits obtained when they were banned.

New York State - 5th Generation and beyond allowed.

Texas - there are areas with restrictions - check your local laws. Not legal in Travis County has been confirmed.

Vermont - F4 and beyond legal only

Washington - there are areas with restrictions - check your local laws.

United Kingdom

It is useful to remind ourselves that some generations of Bengal cats are CITES regulated. This reminds us that the Bengal cat is a wildcat hybrid. It is easy to forget as the Bengal cats we see and those at cat shows are so domesticated.

You have to be a pretty fantastic cat with regard to behavior, never mind appearance, to compete at the cat shows as the cats are handled a lot by strangers.

CITES stands for Convention on International Trade in Endangered Species of Wild Fauna and Flora.

CITES is an agreement between governments who are signed up to the convention. The agreement is designed to protect wildlife by regulating trade in wildlife between these countries.

The ideas for the convention were put forward in the 1960s. The agreement was drafted in 1973 and came into effect in 1975. There are 172 parties to the agreement currently. There are about 189 countries in the world (I say about because "countries" such as the Vatican are an anomaly).

When a country (State) becomes a party it has to enact laws in the country that give effect to the convention. This works in the same way as the European Union. I would have thought that it could be difficult to enforce the agreement and ensure agreeing countries enact the requisite laws and then enforce them.

As Bengal cats come from a true wild cat, the Asian Leopard cat, Bengal cats are CITES regulated. In what way are they regulated? In respect of the UK and EEC countries (as far as I am aware) this is the position:

Fifth (5th) generation Bengal cats (F5) are not regulated by CITES and can enter the UK under the Pet Travel Scheme (see link below). The rules of the scheme must be complied with and the cat should have a proper pedigree certificate from TICA.

Fourth generation (F4) and upwards (F3, F2 and F1) Bengal cats are CITES regulated. This is because CITES regulates hybrid animals whose recent lineage includes certain wild animals as listed in Appendix 1 or 2 of the Convention.

The Asian Leopard cat is listed and up to the fourth generation is considered "recent lineage".

For these Bengal generation cats you'll need an import/export license. There may be health requirements that can be dealt with by The Department for Environment Food and Rural Affairs, (DEFRA).

Defra also enforces the The Dangerous Wild Animals Act 1976. This act by implication only includes the Bengal cat. This probably wasn't intended but at the time the act was drafted the Bengal cat was only just being "created" in the USA.

For many years Bengal cats required a license (technically) but the issuing of a license was and is the responsibility of the local authority that it seems routinely used discretion to wave the need for a license.

As of Oct 2007, the schedule to the The Dangerous Wild Animals Act 1976 has been amended. Defra don't specify exactly that the Bengal cat is excluded from the need for a license (and I have found it hard to research this), but would seem that a license is no longer required. Certainly in practice it wasn't anyway so this simply makes it more formal.

As I said F1-F4 Bengal cats are CITES regulated. A license is required. Click on the link below to read what Defra says about importing pet animals into Britain.

Canada

Alberta - F4 and lower hybrids allowed.

Appendix IV - TICA Bengal Breed Standard

(Source: http://www.tica.org/members/publications/standards/bg.pdf)

HEAD - 35 points
Shape - 6
Ears - 6
Eyes - 5
Chin - 3
Muzzle - 4
Nose - 2
Profile - 6
Neck - 3

BODY - 30 points
Torso - 5
Legs - 4
Feet - 4
Tail - 5
Boning - 6
Musculature - 6

COAT/COLOR/PATTERN - 35 points
Texture - 10
Pattern - 15
Color - 10

CATEGORIES: All DIVISION: Tabby, Silver/Smoke

COLORS:

Brown Tabby, Seal Sepia Tabby, Seal Mink Tabby, Seal Lynx Point, Black Silver Tabby, Seal Silver Sepia Tabby, Seal Silver Mink Tabby, Seal Silver Lynx Point. Spotted or Marbled Patterns ONLY.

PERMISSIBLE OUT CROSSES:

None.

HEAD:

Shape: Broad modified wedge with rounded contours. Longer than it is wide. Slightly small in proportion to body, but not to be taken to extreme. The skull behind the ears makes a gentle curve and flows into the neck.

Allowance to be made for jowls in adult males. Overall look of the head should be as distinct from the domestic cat as possible.

Ears: Medium to small, relatively short, with wide base and rounded tops. Set as much on side as top of head, following the contour of the face in the frontal view, and pointing forward in the profile view. Light horizontal furnishings acceptable; but lynx tipping undesirable.

Eyes: Oval, almost round. Large, but not bugged. Set wide apart, back into face, and on slight bias toward base of ear. Eye color independent of coat color except in the lynx points. The more richness and depth of color, the better.

Chin: Strong chin, aligns with tip of nose in profile.

Muzzle: Full and broad, with large, prominent whisker pads and high, pronounced cheekbones. Slight muzzle break at the whisker pads.

Nose: Large and wide; slightly puffed nose leather.

Profile: Curve of the forehead should flow into the bridge of the nose with no break. Bridge of nose extends above the eyes; the line of the bridge extends to the nose tip, making a very slight, to nearly straight, concave curve.

Neck: Long, substantial, muscular, in proportion to the head and body.

BODY:

Torso: Long and substantial, not oriental or foreign. Medium to large (but not quite as large as the largest domestic breed).

Legs: Medium length, slightly longer in the back than in the front.

Feet: Large, round, with prominent knuckles.

Tail: Medium length, thick, tapered at end with rounded tip.

Boning: Sturdy, firm; never delicate.

Musculature: Very muscular, especially in the males, one of the most distinguishing features.

COAT/COLOR/PATTERN:

Length: Short to medium. Allowance for slightly longer coat in kittens.

Texture: Dense and luxurious, close lying, unusually soft and silky to the touch.

Patterns: Spotted or marbled.

Spotted:

Spots shall be random, or aligned horizontally. Rosettes showing two distinct colors or shades, such as paw print shaped, arrowhead shaped, doughnut or half-doughnut shaped or clustered are preferred to single spotting but not required.

Contrast with ground color must be extreme, giving distinct pattern and sharp edges. Strong, bold chin strap and mascara markings desirable. Virtually white undersides and belly desirable. Blotchy horizontal shoulder streaks, spotted legs and spotted or rosetted tail are desirable. Belly must be spotted.

Marbled:
See TICA Uniform Color Description (74.1.1.2.1).

COLORS:

Brown Tabby:

All variations of brown are allowed. Markings various shades of brown to black. Light spectacles encircling the eyes and a virtually white ground color on the whisker pads, chin, chest, belly and inner legs is desirable.

Seal Sepia Tabby, Seal Mink Tabby, and Seal Lynx Point Tabby:

Pattern can be various shades of brown. There should be very little or no difference between the color of the body (pattern) markings and point color.

GENERAL DESCRIPTION:

The goal of the Bengal breeding program is to create a domestic cat which has physical features distinctive to the small forest-dwelling wildcats, and with the loving, dependable temperament of the domestic cat.

Keeping this goal in mind, judges shall give special merit to those characteristics in the appearance of the Bengal which are distinct from those found in other domestic cat breeds.

A Bengal cat is an athletic animal, alert to its surroundings; a friendly, curious, confident cat with strength, agility, balance and grace. It is a medium to large cat which exhibits a very muscular and solid build. Its wide nose with prominent whisker pads and large oval, almost round eyes in a slightly small head enhance the wild appearance and expressive nocturnal look.

It's very slight, to nearly straight, concave profile and relatively short ears with wide base and rounded tips add to the Bengal's distinctive and unique appearance.

The short, dense coat has a uniquely soft and silky feel. The coat may be glittered or not glittered, with neither type to be given preference. A thick, low-set, medium-length tail adds balance to the cat.

ALLOWANCES:

Smaller size, in balanced proportion, of females. Slightly longer coat in kittens. Jowls in adult males. Eyes slightly almond shaped. Mousy undercoat. Paw pads not consistent with color group description.

PENALIZE:

Spots on body running together vertically forming a mackerel tabby pattern on spotted cats; circular bulls-eye pattern on marbled cats; substantially darker point color (as compared to color of body markings) in Seal Sepia, Seal Mink, or Seal Lynx Point cats. Any distinct locket on the neck, chest, abdomen, or any other area.

WITHHOLD ALL AWARDS:

Belly not patterned.

Temperament must be unchallenging; any sign of definite challenge shall disqualify. The cat may exhibit fear, seek to flee, or generally complain aloud, but may not threaten to harm.

In accordance with Show Rules, ARTICLE SIXTEEN, the following shall be considered mandatory disqualifications: a cat that bites (216.9), a cat showing evidence of intent to deceive (216.10).

Adult whole male cats not having two descended testicles (216.11)

Cats with all or part of the tail missing, except as authorized by a board approved standard (216.12.1)

Cats with more than five toes on each front foot and four toes on each back foot, unless proved the result of an injury or as authorized by a board approved standard (216.12.2)

Visible or invisible tail faults if Board approved standard requires disqualification (216.12.4)

Crossed eyes if Board approved standard requires disqualification (216.12.5), total blindness (216.12.6)

Markedly smaller size, not in keeping with the breed (216.12.9)

Depression of the sternum or unusually small diameter of the rib cage itself (216.12.11.1).

Appendix V - GCCF Bengal Standard (UK)

(Source: http://www.bengalcat.co.uk/Bengal-Cat-Breed-Standards.htm)

Bengal Preliminary Standard of Points

Breed Number 76

Brown (Black) Spotted Bengal 76 / 30

Brown (Black) Marbled Bengal 76 / 20

Blue-Eyed Snow Spotted Bengal 76b / 30

Blue-Eyed Snow Marbled Bengal 76b / 20

AOC-Eyed Snow Spotted Bengal 76a / 30

AOC-Eyed Snow Marbled Bengal 76a / 20

General Type Standard

The Bengal should be alert, friendly and affectionate, and in excellent physical condition, with a dependable temperament.

The Bengal's wild appearance is enhanced by its distinctive spotted or marbled tabby coat which should be thick and luxurious. The Bengal is a large to medium cat, sleek and muscular with a thick tail which is carried low. The female may be smaller than the males.

Head and Neck

Broad medium wedge with round contours, slightly longer than it is wide with high cheekbones. The head should be rather small in proportion to the body but not taken to extremes.

The profile has a gentle curve from the forehead to the bridge of the nose. The nose is large and broad with a slightly puffed nose leather. The muzzle should be full and broad with a slightly rounded, firm chin and pronounced whisker pads created by the widely set canine teeth.

The neck should be thick, muscular and in proportion to the body. Allowance should be made for jowls in adult males.

Ears

Medium to small, rather short with a wide base and rounded tips. Set as much on the side as on the top of the head, following the contour of the face in the front view and pointing forward in profile. Light horizontal furnishings are acceptable, but ear tufts are undesirable.

Eyes

Oval, may be slightly almond shaped, large but not bold. Set on a slight slant towards the base of the ear.

Body

Long, sleek and muscular. Large to medium and robust with the hindquarters slightly higher than the shoulders, showing depth of flank.

Legs and Paws

Legs of medium length, strong and muscular. The hind legs should be a little longer than the front and be more robust. The paws should be large and rounded.

Tail

Medium length, thick and even, with a rounded tip; may be tapered towards the end.

Coat

Short to medium in length, very dense, luxurious and unusually soft to the touch. Allowance should be made for a slightly longer coat in kittens.

Bengal Tabby Descriptions

Spotted Pattern

The spectacles which encircle the eyes should preferably extend into vertical streaks, which may be outlined by an "M" marking on the forehead. Broken streaks or spots run over the head on either side of a complex scarab marking, down the neck and onto the shoulders where they may break up into rosettes.

Rosettes are formed by a part circle of spots around a distinctly lighter centre. Strong, bold chin strap, mascara markings, distinct broken or unbroken necklet(s) and blotchy horizontal shoulder streaks or spots are desirable.

Spots may vary in size or shape but should be generally large, well-formed and distributed at random, or in horizontal alignment. Contrast with the ground colour must be extreme, giving a distinct pattern and a sharp outline to the spots.

Arrowhead-shaped spots are desirable. Larger spots may be rosetted. This is preferable to single spotting but is not essential. The stomach must be spotted (except in Blue-Eyed Snow kittens).

The legs may show broken horizontal lines and/or spots. The tail should have rings, streaks and/or spots along its length, with a solid dark coloured tip. Spots should not run together vertically, forming a mackerel tabby pattern.

Marbled Pattern

The spectacles which encircle the eyes should preferably extend into vertical streaks which may be outlined by an "M" marking on the forehead.

Broken streaks run over the head on either side of a complex scarab marking, down the neck and onto the shoulders. Strong, bold chin straps, mascara markings, distinct broken or unbroken necklet(s) and blotchy horizontal shoulder streaks or spots are desirable.

There should be a distinct pattern with large swirled patches or streaks, clearly defined but not symmetrical, giving the impression of marbled, preferably with a horizontal flow.

Contrast must be extreme with distinct shapes and sharp outlines. The stomach must be spotted (except in Blue-Eyed Snow kittens).

The legs may show broken horizontal lines and/or spots. The tail may be ringed, marbled and/or spotted along its length, with a solid dark coloured tip.

The marbled markings should have as little similarity to the classic tabby as possible. A vertical striped mackerel tabby tendency is also undesirable.

Glossary

A

Ailurophile - An individual who loves cats.

Ailurophobe - An individual exhibiting fear or even hatred of cats.

Allergen - As it relates to cats, the protein Fel d 1, present in the animal's saliva and sebaceous glands, is the primary allergen to which sensitive individuals display an adverse reaction.

Allergy - A sensitivity displayed in individuals to the Fel d 1 protein in cats, generally characterized by sneezing, watering of the eyes, skin rashes, and itches.

Alter - A blanket term describing the spaying or neutering of a companion animal.

B

Bloodline - A line of descent in pedigreed animals that can be verified for genetic purposes.

Breed Standard - As a basis of evaluating a given breed for show purposes, a set of optimum criteria is developed for given physical characteristics and referred to as a "standard."

Breed - A group of cats with similar physical characteristics related by common ancestry that produce like offspring.

Breeder - An individual that works with a specific cat breed, coordinating a reproductive program with dams and sires to improve the genetic quality of the line.

Breeding - The pairing of dams and sires within a breed to produce offspring.

Breeding Program - The selective mating of cats in an organized program for the production of offspring that are superior examples of the breed.

Breed True - The ability of a male and female cat to have offspring that resemble themselves that conform to the standard of the breed.

C

Caterwaul - A discordant feline vocalization that is shrill in nature.

Cat Fancy - A broad term descriptive of the larger body of associations, clubs, groups, and individuals interested in the welfare, breeding, and showing of cats.

Cattery - A facility established to house or breed cats in an organized program.

Certified Pedigree - A registered confirmation of a cat's lineage as affirmed by a recognized feline association.

Coat - An alternate term for the fur of a feline.

Crate - A small container designed to safely convey a domestic pet between locations or as a temporary means of confinement.

Crossbred - The offspring of a dam and sire each of a different breed.

D

Dam - In a parenting set of cats, the female partner, also called the "queen."

Declawing - A surgical procedure to take out a cat's claws permanently. Highly controversial and widely regarded as an act of cruelty.

Domesticated - Tamed animals that work with or live in proximity to humans in a companionable relationship.

E

Exhibitor - The owner of a purebred cat who participates in cat shows organized by a recognized feline organization.

F

Fel d 1 - The protein present in a cat's saliva and sebaceous glands responsible for causing an allergic reaction in some humans.

Feline - Members of the family Felidae. There are seven species of "big" cats and 30 "small" cats.

Flehmening/Flehmen Reaction - When cats open their mouths to draw air over Jacobsen's Organ, two openings in the roof of the mouth that allow the animal to essentially "taste" an odor. The gesture is often mistaken as a grimace or evidence of dislike.

G

Gene pool - The collective genetic information in a population of organisms.

Genes - A DNA sequence occupying a specific area of a chromosome that determines the presence of given characteristics in an organism.

Genetic - Inherited tendencies, characteristics, conditions or traits present in an organism.

Genetics - The scientific study of heredity.

Genotype - The genetic makeup of an organism or a group of organisms.

Guard Hair - The outer layer of a cat's fur comprised of coarser, longer hairs.

H

Heat - In mammals the estrus cycle or "season" of females.

Hereditary - Genetically transmitted diseases, traits, characteristics, or conditions passed from parent to offspring.

Histamine - A physiologically active amine in plant and animal tissue released from mast cells as part of an allergic reaction in humans.

Household Pet - A cat not registered to be exhibited or shown in competition.

Housetraining - The process by which a companion feline is taught to urinate and defecate in a litter box.

I

Immunization - Also referred to as vaccination. A series of shots to inoculate an animal against an infectious disease.

J

Jacobsen's Organ - Two small openings in the roof of a cat's mouth that allow the animal to "taste" a scent.

L

Litter - The number of offspring in a single birth. Generally 3-4 in cats, although 6-10 is not uncommon.

Litter Box - A container used by an indoor cat to urinate and defecate. Filled with commercial kitty "litter" or sand.

N

Neuter - The act of castrating a male cat.

P

Papers - Proof of a cat's pedigree and registration.

Pedigree - The written record of a cat's genealogy going back three or more generations.

Pet Quality - Animals that are not deemed to meet an accepted show standard suitable for exhibition and competition or to participate in an organized breeding program.

Q

Queen - A female cat still capable of reproducing.

R

Rabies - A viral disease that is highly infections and typically fatal to warm blooded animals. It attacks the central nervous system and is transmitted by the bite of an infected animal.

Registered Cat - A cat that is recognized by a feline association via proper documentation of its ancestry.

S

Scratching Post - A tower-like structure covered in carpet or rope that allows a cat to sharpen and clean its claws inside the house without being destructive to furniture.

Secondary Coat - In a cat, the fine hairs of the undercoat.

Show - An organized exhibition in which judges evaluate cats according to accepted standard for each breed and make awards accordingly.

Show Quality - Cats that meet the standards for their breed at a sufficient level to compete in organized cat shows.

Show Standard - A description of the ideal qualities of a breed of cats used as the basis for which the cats are judged in competition. Also known as standard of point.

Sire - The male member of a parenting set of cats.

Spay - The surgery to remove a female cat's ovaries.

Spray - A behavior typically seen in male cats whereby the animal emits a stream of urine as a territorial marker.

Stud - An intact male cat that has not been altered and is used as part of a breeding program.

T

Tapetum Lucidum - The interior portion of a cat's eye that aids in night vision and is highly reflective.

V

Vaccine - A weakened or dead preparation of a bacterium, virus, or other pathogen used to stimulate the production of antibodies for the purpose of creating immunity against the disease when injected.

W

Whole - A cat of either gender that is intact, and has not been neutered or spayed.

Index

Made in the USA
San Bernardino, CA
08 March 2019